All About Money

Savings

Sharon Coan, M.S.Ed.

People go to work.

They **earn** money.

They **save** money.

They put it in the bank.

They **spend** money.

They buy things.

They buy things they want.

They buy books.

They buy bikes.

They go on fun trips.

They buy things they need.

They buy homes.

They buy food.

They buy clothes.

People earn money.

They buy things they
need and want.

List It!

1. Fold a paper in half.

2. Write *needs* on one side.

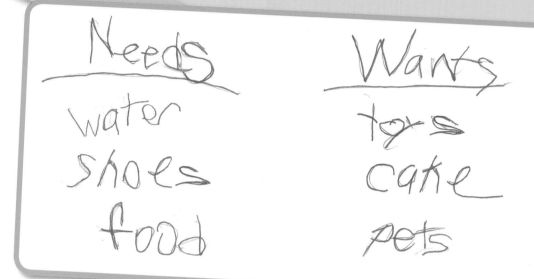

3. Write *wants* on the other side.

4. Write a list of needs and wants.

Glossary

earn—to get something for work you have done

save—to keep and not spend

spend—to use money to pay for something

Index

Your Turn!

People earn money. They can spend it or save it. Tell a friend how people can use money.

Consultants

Shelley Scudder
Gifted Teacher
Broward County Schools

Caryn Williams, M.S.Ed.
Madison County Schools
Huntsville, AL

Publishing Credits

Conni Medina, M.A.Ed., *Managing Editor*
Lee Aucoin, *Creative Director*
Torrey Maloof, *Editor*
Lexa Hoang, *Designer*
Stephanie Reid, *Photo Editor*
Rachelle Cracchiolo, M.S.Ed., *Publisher*

Image Credits: Cover, pp.1, 14 Blue Jean Images/Alamy; pp.2, 7, 10, 12, 15 Blend Images/Alamy; p.16 MBI/Alamy; p.6 Panorama Productions Inc./Alamy; p.9 AE Pictures Inc./ Getty Images; p.23 (bottom) amana images RF/Getty Images; p.23 (top) Cultura/Hybrid Images/Getty Images; p.5 Keith Brofsky/Getty Images; p.11 amriphoto/iStockphoto; p.13 jhorrocks/iStockphoto; p.4 nyul/iStockphoto; p.19 Teacher Created Materials; All other images from Shutterstock.

Teacher Created Materials
5301 Oceanus Drive
Huntington Beach, CA 92649-1030
http://www.tcmpub.com
ISBN 978-1-4333-7348-0